Quotes from some of our famous readers:

"Ho! Ho! Ho!"

Santa Clone

"Everybody must get cloned!
Best book on the subject . . ."

The Rolling Clone

"I've been burning to read this!"

Clone of Arc

"Funnier than the phone book."

"Ma" Bell Teleclone

CLONES I HAVE KNOWN

by Sy Clone

A Tempo Star Book
Distributed by Ace Books
Grosset & Dunlap, Inc., Publishers
New York, N.Y. 10010
A Filmways Company

CLONES I HAVE KNOWN

The Clone Age

"*I vant to be a clone.*"

"It's just a couple o' miles down the road as the clone flies."

The Clone Ranger

Clone Flakes

Crunchy Clonola

"Old King Clone was a merry old soul . . ."

"Need somebody to call my clone."

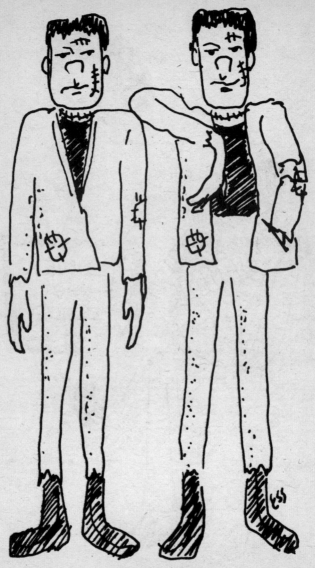

Frankenclone

Teleclone

Sherlock Clones

The Old Folks at Clone

Ice Cream Clone

On the Clonedike Trail

Clone-on-the-Cob

Cloneward Bound

"People in glass houses shouldn't throw clones!"

Cloney Island

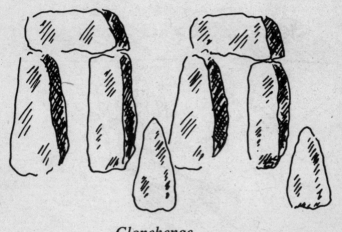

Clonehenge

"Clone, clone on the range"

The Iceman Cloneth

"Send in the Clones"

"*Clona sit right down and write myself a letter . . .*"

Accident-clone

"Clon voyage!"

Clone Shark

"Old Mother Hubbard went to the cupboard to fetch her poor doggie a clone . . ."

"Get a clone, little doggie!"

"*I believe the American people have a have a right
to know whether or not their President is a clone.
Well, I am* not *a clone!*"

Early American Clonial Furniture

Clonedestine Meeting

Off on his clone

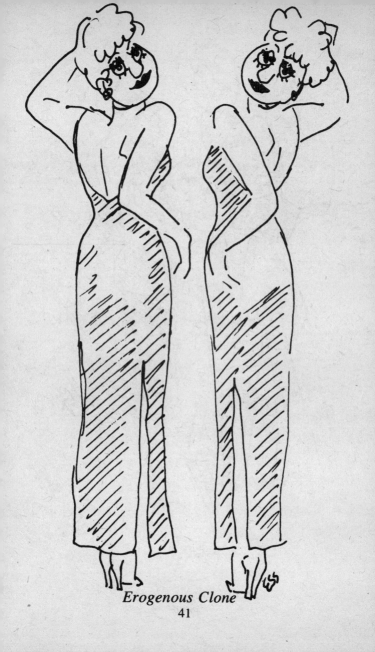

Erogenous Clone

41

Calvin Clone

Skull and Crossclones

Rosemary Cloney

The Clone and I

"A clone is a clone is a clone is a clone is a . . ."

A Thousand Clones

Santa Clone

"*Show me the way to go clone.*"

Clonesome George Gobel

A Clone's Day Journey Into Night

Anna Klonenina

Clone and Dagger

"*Stop cloning around!*"

"*There's* no *place like clone!*"

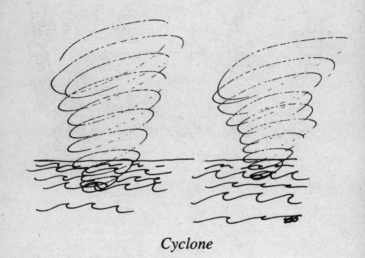

Cyclone

King Clone

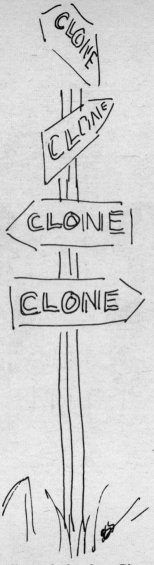

All roads lead to Clone

"*Clone Over Miami*"

The Emperor's New Clones

''Don't you just love *clone as you are parties?*''

"*The answer, my friend, is clone in the wind . . .*"

"Your next stop: The Twilight Clone!"

Clone Fever

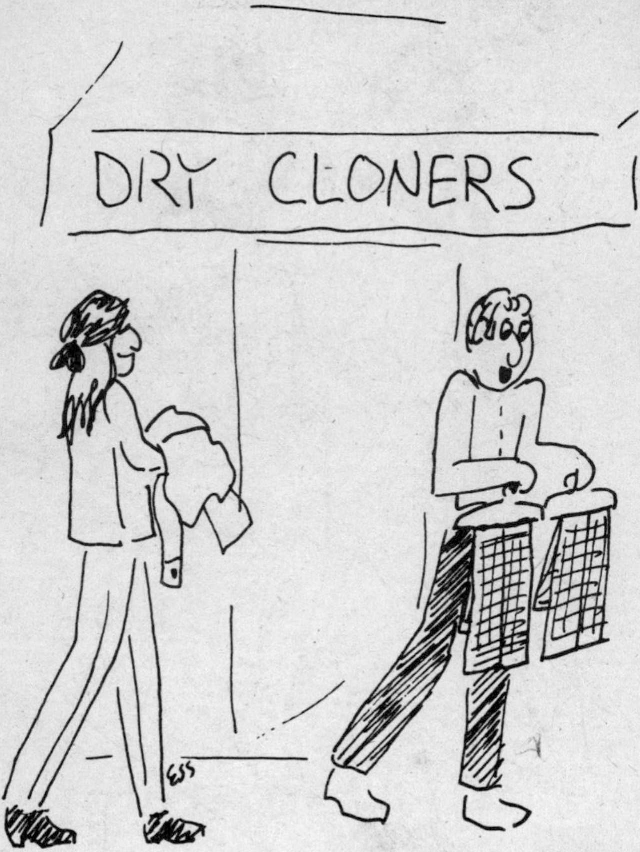
DRY CLONERS
ESS

The Cloneliness of the Long Distance Runner

The Cheese Stands A Clone

Clona Lisa

"Too Tall" Clones

Sgt. Pepper's Clonely Hearts Club Band

Clonedeminium

Clone of Arc

Christopher Clonebus

Don Vito Cloneone

Spring Housecloning

The Clone Star State

"*My, how you've clone!*"

Keeping up with the Cloneses

Mark Anthony and Cloneopatra

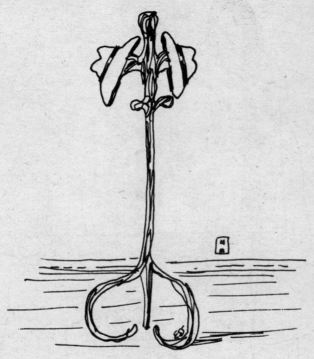

"Any place I hang my hat is clone."

SAVINGS AND CLONE ASSOCIATION

Gclones

Lt. Clonel

''*He's nothing but skin and clones!*''

Fred Flintclone

Cloneo and Juliet

''Won't you come clone Bill Bailey?''

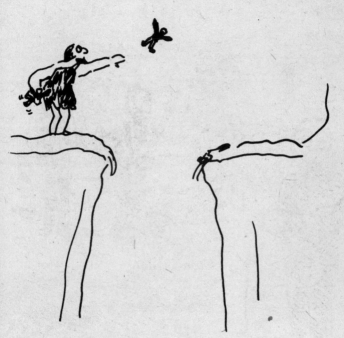

"Just a clone's throw away!"

Clon Vivant

Obscene clone caller

"*Come to me my melancloney baby!*"

Vacuum Cloner

We Are Not Aclone!

Saxoclone

"I think we're a clone now."

Semi-clone

"Clone me a dime?"

All for clone and clone for all!

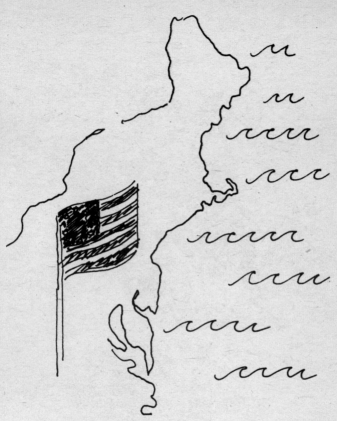

The Original Thirteen Clonies

Pine Clone

It's clonely at the top

"Oh well, to each his clone!"

"Scarface" Al Caclone

A Portrait of the Artist As a Young Clone

Ku Klux Klone

"I've clone accustomed to your face!"

"Boy, did I get cloned last night!"

THE
CLONY
AWARDS

The Clony Express

"Clone wasn't built in a day ya' know!"

Clone deaf

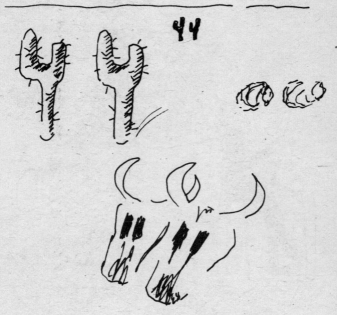

"Bury me not on the clone praireee!"

Clony tail

"C' est si clon!"

Napoleon Clonaparte

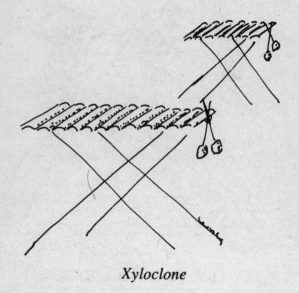

Xyloclone

"A clone at last!"

Megaclone

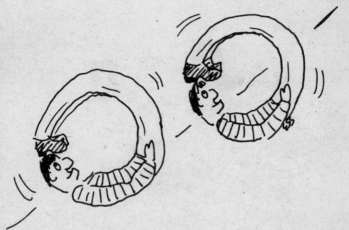

A rolling clone gathers no moss.

Frosty the Cloneman

"How would you like to be Clone for a Day!"

Walter Clonkite

"Everybody *must get cloned!*"

Sink like a clone

Abraham Linclone

Coca Clona

Long Clone Silver

Dunkin' Clonut

Demilitarized Clone

Chili Clon Carne

Clonewall Jackson

Lassie Come Clone

The Cloneheads

"Here today . . . . Clone Tomorrow!"

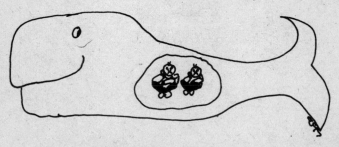

Clonah and the Whale

"She'll be clonin' 'round the mountain . . ."

Cloni Home Permanent

The Clone Room

"You'll never walk a clone!"

"Clon Appetit!"

Clone Baez

Clone With The Wind

C.O.D. (Clone On Delivery)

Laugh Clone, Laugh

Clone Chowder

Old Clones

"That's *no lady,* that's *my clone!*"

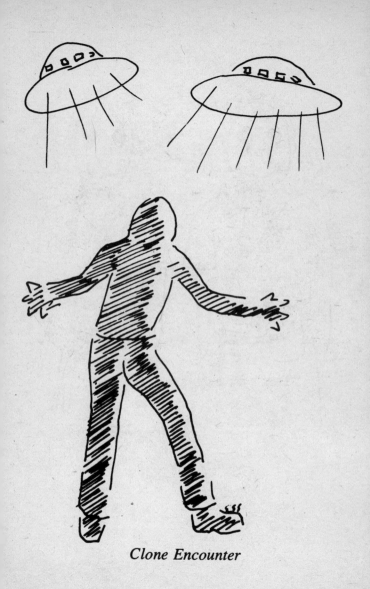

Clone Encounter

I, Clonius

"Heeeeere's Cloney!"

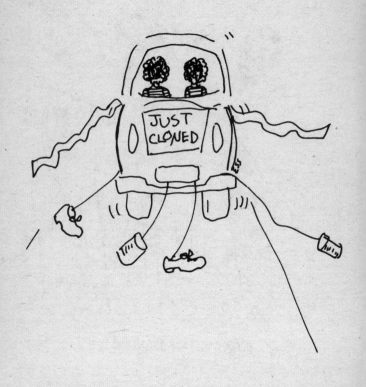

CLONE YOUR OWN

Connect the Dots

ABOUT THE AUTHOR

Sy Clone was born in Bora Bora in 1818. After a brief stint as a tutu salesman, he moved to Walla Walla, and lived quietly with his dog, Toto. Unfortunately, in 1919, he was bitten by a tse-tse fly and contracted beri beri simultaneously. During a drug induced fever he did not write "Promises, Promises" nor "I Do, I Do." He did, however, move to New York, New York where he got a job as a bailiff because of his ability to shout *Oyez, Oyez* when the judge entered the courtroom. He is presently serving concurrent life sentences at Sing Sing where he is visited regularly by his wife, Mary Mary (the gardening expert). This is one of his two books, the other being the same.

Clone Tee Shirts

Now that you've been clone away by the book, you can order tees for clones you've known! Design features title with Clone Ranger, Clone Encounter and others. Navy on Lt. Blue. Specify S-M-L-XL.

Clone Tee Shirts

P.O. Box 94 , Cambridge, MA O2142